P9-CEZ-928

The Way I Act

Verses by Steve Metzger

Illustrations by Janan Cain

Parenting Press, Inc.

Seattle, Washington

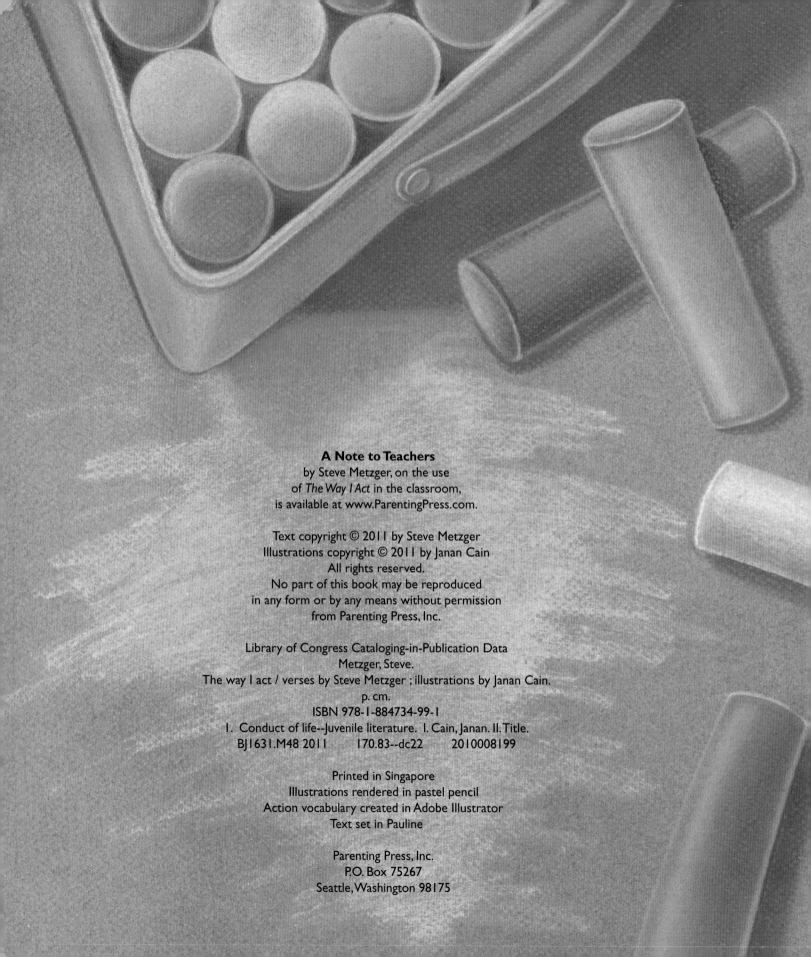

A Note to Teachers
by Steve Metzger, on the use
of The Way I Act in the classroom,
is available at www.ParentingPress.com.

Library of Congress Cataloging-in-Publication Data
Metzger, Steve.
The way I act / verses by Steve Metzger ; illustrations by Janan Cain.
p. cm.
ISBN 978-1-884734-99-1
1. Conduct of life--Juvenile literature. I. Cain, Janan. II. Title.
BJ1631.M48 2011   170.83--dc22   2010008199

Printed in Singapore
Illustrations rendered in pastel pencil
Action vocabulary created in Adobe Illustrator
Text set in Pauline

Parenting Press, Inc.
P.O. Box 75267
Seattle, Washington 98175

To Ilse Metzger
(my mother)
and Mutti (my grandmother)
and William Stern (my uncle),
three extraordinarily
brave people
—S.M.

For my nieces and nephews—
Ryan, Paige, Jessica,
Danielle, Taylor, Paul, Kara,
Katelyn, Doreen, Michael,
Sam, Mick, Rachel,
Olivia, Ben, Pat, Grace
and Emma
—J.C.

Special thanks to Emily & Isabella Cain and Erica Fong for posing for the illustrations.

Curious

What planet is the biggest?

Where do wild geese fly?

I want to learn about the world,

I'm **curious**, that's why!

I do my homework

every night,

Responsible

I fix my sister's sled.

I'm proud when

I'm **responsible**,

I even make my bed!

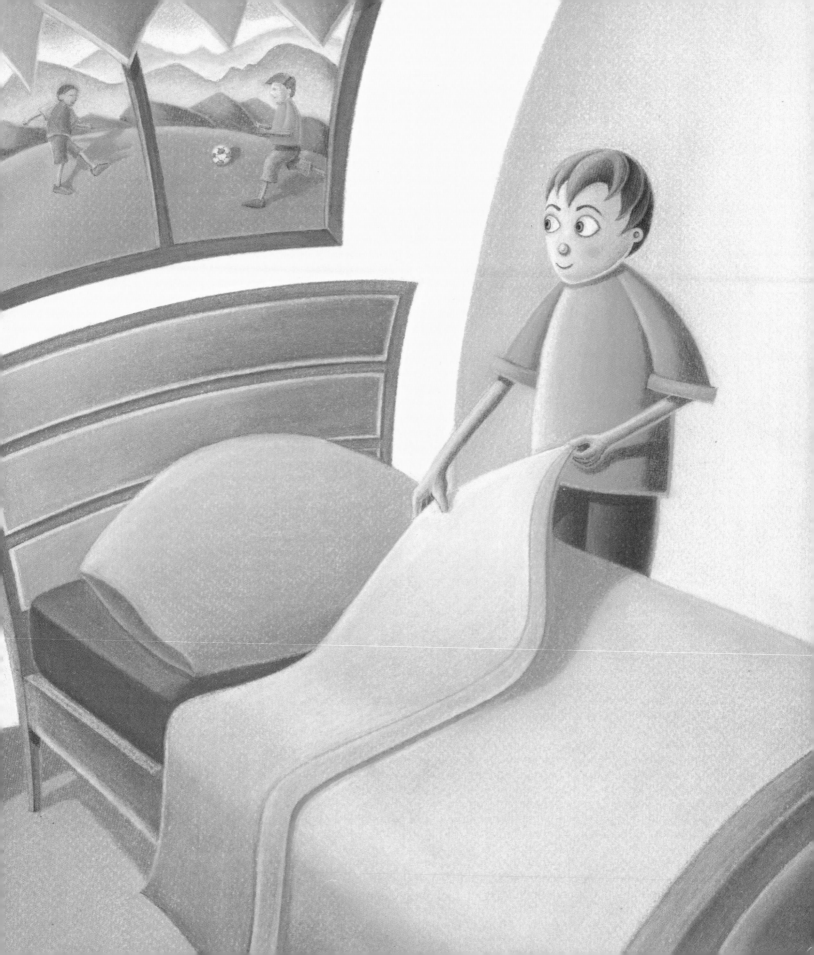

Compassionate

When Grandma's sad, I hold her hand. I help friends when they fall.
I'm **compassionate** when I care for creatures great and small.

I do not take what

isn't mine,

Trustworthy

When tempted

I walk on by.

I'm **trustworthy**,

I tell the truth,

Even when

I'd rather lie.

BRAVE!

I'm **brave** when I get on the bus,

And I go off to school.

I'm brave when I try skating,

Or jump into the pool.

No matter if you're shy or bold,

I hope you'll play with me.

Let's read or draw or climb a tree.

I'm **friendly** as can be.

Hooray for me! This puzzle's done!

Now all the pieces fit!

Be **persistent**, that's my goal,

I'll try hard not to quit!

Persistent

I honor

my parents'

requests.

When asking

I say, "Please."

I know that I'm

respectful, too,

When I

don't push

or tease.

RESPECTFUL

Cooperative

I pass the ball

in soccer games,

I help you fly

your kite.

When we are

cooperative,

We don't have

time to fight.

CAPABLE

I can do

so many things,

Like sweep

and sing and run.

It's great

to be so **capable**.

I smile

and say,

"Well done!"

Dancing! Prancing! Running! Jumping!

Spinning like a top.

When I'm **active**, I feel GREAT!

And never want to stop.

Considerate

I'm **considerate** of other kids,

I do not scream or hit.

When Grandpa needs a chair, I say,

"Here's a comfy place to sit."

I'm a wizard; I'm a star,

I play until I'm done.

I love to be **imaginative**,

My games are so much fun!

Imaginative

Friendly, brave, considerate,

Curious, on the go.

My actions show who **I am** now,

And how I want to grow!

A Note to Parents

The Way I Act helps children recognize and appreciate their positive actions.
It is the companion book to *The Way I Feel*, a book to help children understand a variety of feelings.
The Way I Act focuses on the choices children make for their behavior. Our goal is to give you an
enjoyable starting place for you and your child to explore actions: how, why,
and when your child does what he does and what the results are.
We invite you to consider these suggestions:

1
Talk about the difference between feelings and actions.
Assure your child that all her feelings are acceptable and ask what emotions she felt today.
Did her feelings lead to actions? What were the consequences of those actions?

2
Make it personal.
As you read this book, ask your child if he has ever acted as the child in the poem does.
Talk about the many different ways one can act in a friendly, or compassionate,
or brave (or other) manner.

3
Invite action.
Make a list of all the positive actions you and your child can think of.
Ask her to tell you about a time she acted in any of those positive ways and how she felt as
a result. Can she tell you how others around her felt, too?

4
Develop judgment.
An older child is ready to think about how hard it can be to decide
what positive action to take in a situation. If Grandma gives him a gift he doesn't like,
should he act in a considerate manner and tell her he likes it?
Or should he act in an honest and practical manner and tell her he would prefer something else
and ask if he could exchange it? Help your child develop judgment.

— Steve Metzger and Janan Cain